E
A
R
T
H
W
O
R
K
S

Chris Collins

THISTLEDOWN PRESS

Canadian Cataloguing in Publication Data

Collins, Chris, 1961-

Earthworks

(New leaf editions)
Poems.
ISBN 0-920633-72-2

I. Title. II. Series

PS8555.0445R3 1990   C811'.54   C90-097082-0
PR9199.3.C64R3 1990

Book design by A.M. Forrie
Cover illustration by Jacqueline Forrie
Graphite drawing by Frances E. Buchan

Typeset by Thistledown Press
Printed and bound in Canada by
Hignell Printing Ltd., Winnipeg

Thistledown Press Ltd.
668 East Place
Saskatoon, Saskatchewan
S7J 2Z5

Acknowledgements

Some of the poems have appeared in *FreeLance, Quarry, Briarpatch* and *NeWest Review.*

The author wishes to acknowledge the financial assistance of the Banff Centre School of Writing in helping to make some of the poems in this book possible. The author also wishes to thank Glen Sorestad, Anne Szumigalski, Patrick Lane and Don Coles for editorial assistance.

This book has been published with the assistance of The Canada Council and the Saskatchewan Arts Board.

for family and friends

CONTENTS

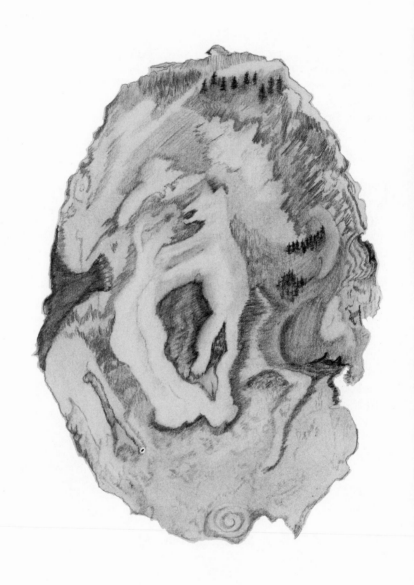

think of
the marks on this page
as wild
pawprints in snow

I make no promises
of destination
within their loops
only
that something intangible
was here
now
(or is it
already then?)
and has
for an instant
clawed
struggled
and dissolved
all before you blink

before I learned to write

I paced barefoot
across cold stone

thick hair clung in patches
along my spine

I loped past words
camouflaged in blood

I could not make fire

I sit
feeding alligators in my notebook
eyes rolled back
costume pupils aimed politely
while rubber ears appear to
intercept wise words

and I bought this outfit
second-hand after learning
see-jack-and-how-fast-jack-runs
a special system
programmed to mirror each mentor
and respond precisely
as expected
it is completely automatic
another welcome
labour-saving device
to allow me to roam
mountains in your classes

and with this year's model
so advanced
I dare you to distinguish
those learning
from those skinny dipping
in deep
moss-lipped pools

a face

in passing

a love   utterly consuming
lasting

four seconds

read read read
Nietzsche's drumstick stuck in my windpipe
I clear my throat
upchuck half-digested philosophers
who ramble round furniture legs
balloon the ceiling until
windows explode wisdom

tell me, do you read this
on the Day of the Dead?
does an iguana cling to your shoulder
stare at a prehistoric plaza?

I hope you are well

please send me a quartz crystal
torn from the heart of a Mayan pyramid

do toreadors really slash bull's genitals?

things are much the same here

last night I saw Bogart in
'The Treasure of the Sierra Madre'

slanting sunrays
coloured the frost fallow land violet
against the fiery red-orange
of the elevator
wind strummed the telephone line
and carried the cold
to numb my cheek

a flap of birds
came towards me
steering the all-bending wind
their shadows passed
but a wood-flesh thud
sounded over the thick whine
a soft, grey body
twirled from the pole
after three dry whispers
its broken body still
creeping blood covered the open beak

and I stood over it
until the bitter cold urged me to walk on
past fight
and cackling squabble
of five jostling magpies
feasting in this warm, feathered meat

we hate one another
and before dawn drive over thirty miles
to this isolated field
crouch a hundred yards apart
holding guns
to shoot over each other's head

feeling as father and son

we sight lines into the grey
fire to clear the air
of bats
between the blinded positions

dropping them without a thought

two wooden cathedrals rise
pull us near the dead/dying
hamlet of Goodeve

spires command flats
stab the immense space with a fervent old faith
invite us to apprehend mystic bell-tower heights

scarved Ukrainian women pass
stoop across empty mainstreet
to observe Lent
beneath gilt-ablaze holy
Slavic domes reflecting
cold sun off iced fields

white winds have brought
colour to my eyes
and skin which is already tinged
with the desperate beauty of autumn
dry leaves
fall with the wind
leaving an edgeless trunk
gumsealed at the ends

now pupils grown over
leaving me blind
I wait for snow
sleepy in the sensation
of warm sap gathering
between my toes

clock ticks
over the sound
of my breathing

wind grinds the corners
of my house
round   (this does not bother me
you see   I have given up
caring)

before long
the ache of this
silent space   my land
will be gone

in this chair
work-taut muscles
loosen   flaccid strands of barbed wire
hanging

I slowly
meet earth   deadfall

join
this silent space

become part

prairie

the question

diary of a farm wife
newsprint school scribbler
fading pencil scrawl
in thirty years
style never changes
brown on brown

darning Ian's socks
selling eggs in the city for extra cash
working the garden
tending children
a practical woman's record
weapon to shrink the horizon

no inkling
the life between the lines
statistics
define her place among the seasons

final entry:
first crow, March 14
19 days early this year

I watch another worker bend
unearth sod easily, drape
grass over each forearm, amass
horizons of turf, expression
calm as his eyes travel
up levels of the palette
this plain icon of sorts, this
green business

it's a dot the spot in your life
you start the change
from a slow, sloth-like
but sure state of dream
to deal in flashing figures
theories and ideas
that, to see
needs be to stare
and burrow with your mind
until a sky-whole view of things
is almost lost
to a pinhole star of light

become delight
to see that kid
stepping, dare-devil style
along the rail-line and looking
between its ties
for agates, Indian hammerheads
anything of interest and
watch him stop
before he sees me looking
to gaze at a moon
in the heat and prairie-blue sky
of this, his summer

televised live to the Woolco foodbar
miles above the whorling hot-dog warmer
a shuttle pilot somersaults in his 10 million dollar
'Manned Maneuvering Unit'
then Reagan appears proposing a space station before '94
while I pay, then step aboard the escalator
rising above shoppers and neon
past fountains and planters up—
up towards the artificial skylight
the muzak swells
and god, Ronald, our future is here

out of sunday morning television he appears
arms upraised, gold ringfingers glittering
captivating my drowsiness
projected is a Florida-tan exuberance
preaching *Self, help yourself* the length of his
fluorescent cathedral
and from here the eyes appear rolled upward
whites gleaming the beneficence
of a God inherent in the devout investor
while blinding, the choir smiles
swaying idyllic-young —his sidearms
out it comes at you
leaning perfect
spreading thick and radiant its own creation

Utopia must be here
since our postman asks
"any trouble with the French Surrealists?"
while handing over bills and coupons

a busdriver with Junior Mints and Thucydides
on the dash
Debussy in a Walkman

and at Safeway a boy bags groceries
while quoting a Stoic philosopher
"adapt yourself to the environment in which
your lot has been cast and show true love
to the fellow mortals with whom
destiny has surrounded you"
with that voice's profile, Marcus Aurelius
tattooed on a forearm flying over broccoli
two thousand years dead and orating above my Oreos
competing with the beep and computer-monotone
of the talking register

"Utopia must be here," I remark at Ultracuts
and she responds, blowdrying with a degree in Sociology
"Oh, let's do a study. Trim the sideburns?"

lycra-suited Olympic bobsledders
chute at 70 miles per hour
through the window of Granada TV Rental
while we stamp, shiver waiting for the bus

(helmeted Russians this run, push-trot alongside
then leap aboard their cherry snowship
centripetally whipped towards the camera . . .)

this city storefront, and a joking boy
who flattens back his cheeks at his friend
hilariously grinning at the G's the sledders
must be pulling

(a gleaming-blue French ship rears on one runner
snow-spraying and jostling down on . . .)

a girl beside me, watching too
her reflection is cold, beautifully
flushed as her eyes glint in passing headlights

(crouched Americans drop, hurtling . . .)

at another, older individual who sets down groceries
eyes his watch, wonders "a strange sport"
while clapping chilled hands in the blue light

(my bus roars away, we accelerate . . .

'I like flowers, so bea-ut-iful'
his every word's an invocation
at six years he hasn't learned
our pronunciations
he watches me prune his magic
gathers the fallen lilacs
mixes them with powdered brick
'love potion?' I ask, busy
'what you think it is,' he says

Gary Numan nihilistic synth
lamenting whine of machine men
(you romantics ohsoboring)
powersurge from chrometurning
walkman hones reflexflare
(away others adeptly strive away ohtobeinhuman)
animal flashdefence/escape
microseconds prohibit pain
thought superseded in neuroelectronic
dance photohorizons
and the quarters repeat
laserlight reflecting in
cateyes
narrowed upon cleankills
as world/screen clears   emptiness

clankgliding by
fromturret Israeli tankommander phonespeaks to gunner
sodeathpole swivels with cameraeye
(crew's powerthrillitch smallseems less voicecause)

ghurkas browsethru leftarmour   exocets   grossrep10mil-
lion
(small facesave less pumpspeak for H.M. overdrawn)

from hilltank suburbs spread scene universal for
(closeup) dirty shoppingcentre artilleryspray
(soundown stifles ragecries   deathanthems
arcadelike roarless shellspurts)

descending spaceshuttle
white Disney cruisemissile   (full test laserload)
cheering Winnebagos   Reagansmile
behindgrin silos   (between   the words
rambling sense in the non)

last night you and I were
night watchmen miles apart, walking
tunnels of a nuclear reactor
radioactive, it's
the only job we can find

I try to listen to my dreams

and get up for factory labour
as you do
two thousand miles away
the tunnel distance
of my dream

I try to listen to my dreams

and riding the subway after work
think of you, when
still tasting canteloupe
from lunch come
associations

the watermelon we'd won
guessing its weight, that summer
you were six, I was ten
its ten pounds six ounces
light
between us

whirring, spitting chainsaw to hand, we harvest
(while
standing back I see
the butterfly
quietly flapping
on your white cotton workcap)

there is something strange about
the way things appear

these objects on the cloth are more than tools

now folds, the shading makes them shapes
in their own right

that when we obtain a confidence, they might

tell me their names

to hide in the abstract
or step out swinging
a freeway under each arm

it's one or the other

or somewhere between head and heart
like this morning
the old woman slowly
picking and eating crabapples
at a bus stop

a man watches a hawk
perching his face sharp into what he sees
as the deaf mute beside
seems so much of where he's grown up
this silent space out the window which speaks
sharp gestures of weather
its mouth always closed

the only two people close to me
we're looking out
picking up bits of the distance
wishing it to show itself
smooth as our faces

crowd, we're watching a man fall
a thousand feet, slow-motion
spume of red smoke from his
heart? (while above us, the chutist balances
checklists, forces, speeds; an aerial
dynamics

involving his body) while

we, the crowd, we dream
all-air, where throwing ourselves   out

we spring the lock

across the street, thirteen storeys up
on a balcony a women exercises
bent at the waist, head bobbing
over morning traffic, vertigo

she's crazy, first to be hanging
her eyes, her long hair, throwing
her breasts to the street, and

second, they say she's slightly
off to begin with, an artist living
alone and beautiful, thirteen storeys
up, I've heard she has terrible

fits of joy as she paints her
body and, falling onto canvas
outlines herself, a splash of colour

it's all he can do to kill himself
Narcissus with a hard-on
head-first through a sheet of glass
end of myth

with her
walking off to sleep around
real pricks in her head
not the sharp sound of his face at the shatter

so freedom goes
always a killing
lightness of bones bagged about in waiting
for a dance

in the new improved country
a power to hold what you don't know
an abstract on the inside
pink of eyelids

I struggle to wish my body back
you have it, are keeping it safe
dress me in doll clothes; I do you
close up we strip each other, smile

I am faced with your grin, it leans
in the door offering a bowl, seems we
can't get by without loving it, the toll
paid both ways; an unreasonable pull

let me murder you, suicide loose
put a needle in our hearts; spells
melting as wax to form figures again
an eye for an eye, in each other's

the moon is full again, unhinged
another eyelid opening in the brain
drinking everything in sight, still
empty and feeling it; pursuit

by what? we could talk about
daquiris and quitting cigarettes
but for the moon, a mallet
cratering love, hammering calm

subtlety is a step in the grave
we spill and the waiter returns
what is lost; who can tell?
tequila is beyond thirst, earth

son and I sit on a glacier
with pencil and ruler
plotting meteors
onto a circle of paper
weighted down against the wind

northern lights are in the way
and the ice is moving
so it's hard to be accurate

he hasn't the patience
wanders off to climb a cliff
hangs by a fingertip
pulling fossils with his teeth

another star falls
I draw it for him
wave that it's time to go
almost too light to see

he returns carrying my skull
a thousand years old

'I howl at the moon
with all my heart
and put the blame
on the dogs'
                    - Rilke

the dog is a man forgetting things
a man missing hands
yes, the dog is a man
on the couch dreaming
brown, the gristle
itch of holes

who do I fool? the dog
is dog, *Canis*
lupus on my couch —the crouch
of dumb blood gnashing

in booze, smoke, my own
hand I am not
beaten, hold the stick
howling "fetch
kill, fetch, kill—
so which dog are we going to be?"

in the laugh, the twist
of man and dog
man and dog and leash
dragging us somewhere
same streets. the bridge. I am

lifting the man free; it's mime
his four legs in air, hands
dropping gestures

my father is all I haven't learned
simpler to escape than understand

he is the calm trap of households
a cell the length of a marriage
a suburb of televisions
sputtering the anthem to an empty couch

he is my fear of becoming round
of falling in love with circles

while he is myself waiting with something to say
in the doorway
finally free of angles

PASSING BY THE PRISON
FOR THE CRIMINALLY INSANE

I strain to glimpse wild eyes
popping in and out of view
mysterious loonies
waddling chimps
the people from my dreams

imagine guards in pointed riding boots
timed scuttling up with a jacket
to throw over the barbs   a contest
could be baseball camp

but the windows are empty
or They stare without moving
no one plays ball in the yard
I hurry by
thinking of zoos
and the soft eyes of lions

made of blades of glass
thus I can see myself
right through
more than one can say of my maker
to whom I pray
rubbing his head between my legs

here comes a girl with a flower
so whole
both of these things
our reflections looking up from the well
something wrong
in this picture
I throw her in to live with it

on I recur
remaking master in his
dreams stitched from bolts
of lightning
I ricochet black

fluid, like finned levers of muscle
the whales revolve
about the small
blue centrifuge of their tank

the merest slide-cell of ocean
to them
their great torpedo bodies
and brains daily bludgeoned
by this circle of habit, this sonar
of the mad

proud thrash of their arms, like ours
underwater, under-
the-skin where
five tiny fingers make a hand, a

fist

you have to free-rent yourself, I'd felt
make room in the big house, opening
more windows for the cat to leap

a packrat showed me this, carousing
it had bad teeth and more stories
than the moth I held closed in a book

that night —it bit into other things
making themselves up as I went, whole
families came in and out, more alive
it seemed to me, watching their pores
girls under the window felt the moon
straddled their bicycles, then rode off

my smoke threw itself away, following

the rat came back to sing me asleep
left droppings and instructions for use

you can't kick a statue in the balls, god knows
I have and only
hurt myself then history, in particular
a toe

though something's got to give, as I know
folk who eat
dust all week and work for it
our immigrants
mostly soul and loving, mind you, simply
as they're wise

to history
to hardship, to the statue wearing brass

she stands on a hill of sand
at home with the sun
hair a wisp of gold on her cheek
half-turned to a sea of trees
stretching to the grass of our birth

at least it's *my* beginning
she offers
I have no idea where she's from
no idea and I am
only an eye dreaming her

woman gesturing across
oceans and valleys curving
out around geological time
'there is start and finish'
she points where I
can see only her
am only an eye dreaming her

you don't want me to idealize
the roses that spring from your closet
that's rough as to say I love you
which won't fool the fish
darting about the sky you augur for truth

as we are in your Persian carpet
where the dragons wind into flowers
breaking the sea for air
we wear nothing but your hair
falling deeper into design

I've got a bird for you
it swims the wild in our eyes
for joy or pain but then perhaps you know
how it goes
in and out of the intricate lie

there's a sentimental
bone in my throat
round as a baby's arm
making a poem with wooden blocks

love comes out
rampant as Christmas
a smile at nothing
wrappings

how can I say you
lover by the window
I lie
like the housecat with its purr

can we hold each other
in words
teach me
to peel an orange with your teeth

once in a small café, I closed my eyes
my world became a head of hair, your smile
a soft rain between our eyes, as we lied

where we first met, shy with coffee
feet touching under the table, at closing
wondering where to take it, the feeling

in the café, I've forgotten where you're from
some place in the sun, was it Arkansas
you told me about, through the skin

it hurts to have nothing left, a quarter
to short the bus, ride home in a mist
of past places I've been, it's three A.M.

the time when I hold your
exact shapely breath
easing into this one room
I could launch into nothing
but your soapsmell
and underneath your heartsmell
between these even walls
timing the beat of our eyes

after a year apart, after the fear
love becomes
running free of itself
I see now my old lover, singing
at washing her skirts
by herself along the weir

born and immediately
married, how we
gave and gave and ate ourselves
beautifully too
close to the bone

not knowing better
then, and what's to know
in one room rejoicing
whole heart in its eye until
even light uncouples

as tonight up
late with an edible moon
my heart a wide
and wiser gyroscope

the same as
different as
hers

Sally and I
on our backs in wet grass
watching the aurora
slide, coil about stars
then retreat up the Amazon

and more stars

I pass the bottle, listening
for supernovas
listening to Sally think

and Sally isn't thinking
is head-stretched
like a moonshot of faith
she's gone off
with a range for everything

saying there are people
upon planets
about stars count the stars

last night we loved
like two bees
all sting and tingling skin

and all day
today I've been humming
at work
in a field of please
a field
magnetic with bees
their sunny buzz and circuitry

I hum to them
my bees
homecoming with pollen
my bees and I
our socks stuffed with gold

you left the door open
'til flies came in with flowers
shrill condolences
I was of two minds to accept
or swat
so I read a lot
ran out and bought
A Field Guide to Mythic Wildlife
and through flora and fauna
tracked you down
to a species —the pushmepullyou
strange as the two of us
put together

she strides with her life behind her
trailing
like the tail of a comet
she its head
all memory, all fiery ball

bursting up the hill with her cane
ladling
like a bee's tongue
bud-to-bud through flowering
all the various
green underthings of spring, gone

and returned like family, the generations
renewing
this life-
long wedding with the earth, this nectar

you have unearthed me

with your tiny pick and
feather duster
my structure succumbs
to familiarity

the delicate brushing
of your fingertips
stimulates the fossil flesh
eyes roll in sockets
make grinding sound
stone mortar and pestle

your tongue dislodges sediment
from between my calcified teeth
which gleam like the surface
of a blind man's eye

and before long
we become a rare geologic formation
for the textbooks

such a mountain making love

brown limbs with a sheen of
sweat on the sand where we
lie, talking about the Bible
find an Indian artifact and
touch the crystalline arrow point
that the blue sky shimmering
overhead is only the release
rousing your nipples taut
in the moment of this arrow
and your blood so smoothly
blessed with an infinite heat

along the river lies a man
and another, and another
I'm finding them in pieces
bits of flint from arrows
the man's made and lost
made and lost with time

it's summer on brown grass
old blood and rosehips
into beaks of waxwings
no slowing to beauty
the geese and gulls calling
mid-river on the mud

but I've come for the man
stones sparked from his hand
quartz, chert, and agate
splinters of what we see
together walking the river
he and I and land

my
neck
aches from
searching for telegraph
chips in stone

I am the missing point
you
are the body of this place

wherein one perfect spear
we touch

who dreamt this card house
and so with cranes, tottered it up
to shine and why? I'd like to know
city-centred in glare
dissonance and speed, all things
reeling, jarring in
to where I keep my peace

I know a man who speaks crow, blackbird
crow to crows
not of this earth, and like
any crow which homes to his land
a still place
full of trees and meats
for silence, like the man himself

and as the lake is sound for silence
and the drum
about to beat with wings, this man

shall stand softly
through all the crow's schuss and need